How to use this dictionary

This book is full of useful words in both Mandarin and English. The English word appears first, followed by the Mandarin word. Look below each Mandarin word for help to sound it out. Try reading the words aloud.

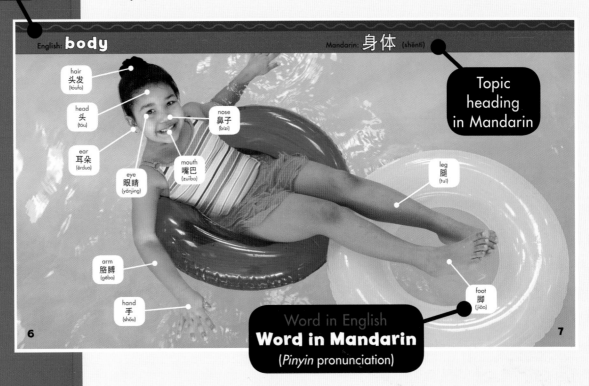

Topic heading in English

English: **body**

Mandarin: 身体 (shēntǐ)

Topic heading in Mandarin

hair
头发
(tóufa)

head
头
(tóu)

nose
鼻子
(bízi)

ear
耳朵
(ěrduo)

eye
眼睛
(yǎnjing)

mouth
嘴巴
(zuǐba)

leg
腿
(tuǐ)

arm
胳膊
(gēbo)

hand
手
(shǒu)

foot
脚
(jiǎo)

6

7

Word in English
Word in Mandarin
(*Pinyin* pronunciation)

Notes about the Mandarin Chinese language

Pinyin is a system of writing Chinese that spells out the sounds of the words using Roman letters. Most of the *Pinyin* pronunciations can be read like English. A few letters have different sounds. Below are some additional pronunciations to help.

| **q** (ch) | **z** (dz) | **e** (uh) | **ui** (way) |
| **x** (sh) | **zh** (dge) | **u** (oo) | **ü** (eu) |

Pinyin also uses four tones. These tones mean that vowel sounds can be said in different ways.

ā, ē, ī, ō, ū = high-level tone, slightly higher than regular speech

á, é, í, ó, ú = rising tone, sound rises like when asking a question

ǎ, ě, ǐ, ǒ, ǔ = dipping tone, sound falls and then rises

à, è, ì, ò, ù = falling tone, starts high and then falls

uncle
叔叔
(shūshu)

mother
妈妈
(māma)

cousin
堂弟
(táng dì)

aunt
婶婶
(shěnshen)

baby
宝宝
(bǎo bǎo)

My First Book of
Mandarin
Chinese Words

by Katy R. Kudela

Translator: Translations.com

apple
苹果
(píngguǒ)

raintree

...any — publishers for children

Contents

grandmother
祖母
(zǔmǔ)

father
爸爸
(bàba)

grandfather
祖父
(zǔfù)

brother
哥哥
(gēge)

sister
妹妹
(mèimei)

hair
头发
(tóufa)

head
头
(tóu)

nose
鼻子
(bízi)

ear
耳朵
(ěrduo)

mouth
嘴巴
(zuǐba)

eye
眼睛
(yǎnjing)

arm
胳膊
(gēbo)

hand
手
(shǒu)

leg
腿
(tuǐ)

foot
脚
(jiǎo)

pyjamas
睡衣
(shuìyī)

coat
外套
(wàitào)

shorts
短裤
(duǎn kù)

boot
靴子
(xuēzi)

8

shoe
鞋
(xié)

hat
帽子
(màozi)

trousers
裤子
(kùzi)

sock
袜子
(wàzi)

dress
连衣裙
(liányīqún)

shirt
衬衫
(chènshān)

9

kite
风筝
(fēngzheng)

doll
洋娃娃
(yángwáwa)

puzzle
拼图
(pīntú)

train
火车
(huǒchē)

wagon
推车
(tuīchē)

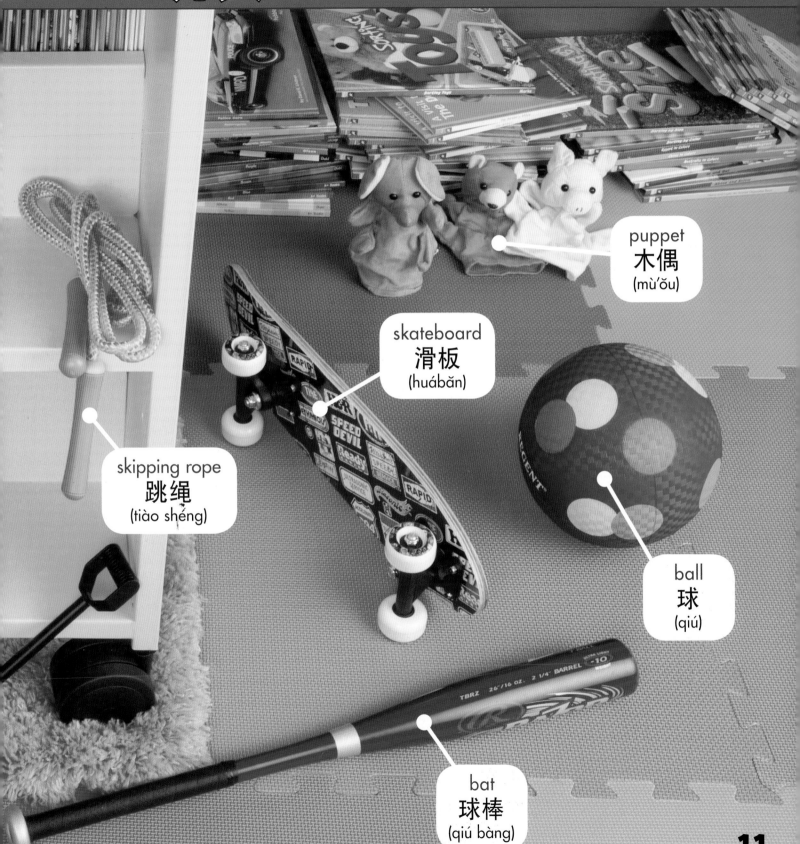

puppet
木偶
(mù'ǒu)

skateboard
滑板
(huábǎn)

skipping rope
跳绳
(tiào shéng)

ball
球
(qiú)

bat
球棒
(qiú bàng)

picture
图画
(túhuà)

lamp
灯
(dēng)

window
窗
(chuāng)

chest of drawers
梳妆台
(shuzhuangtái)

curtain
窗帘
(chuānglián)

blanket
毯子
(tǎnzi)

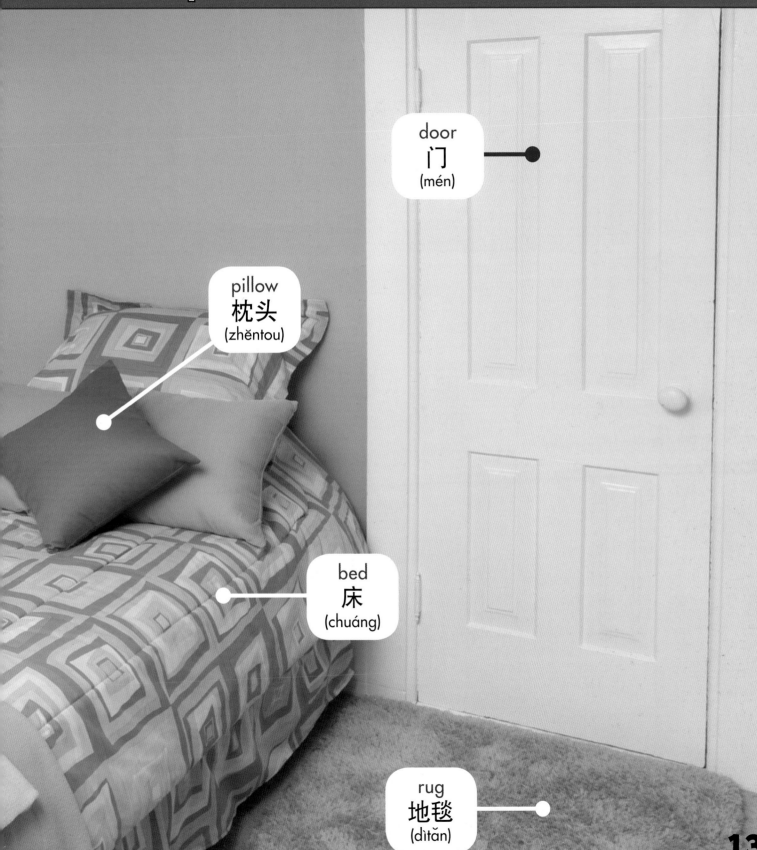

door
门
(mén)

pillow
枕头
(zhěntou)

bed
床
(chuáng)

rug
地毯
(dìtǎn)

13

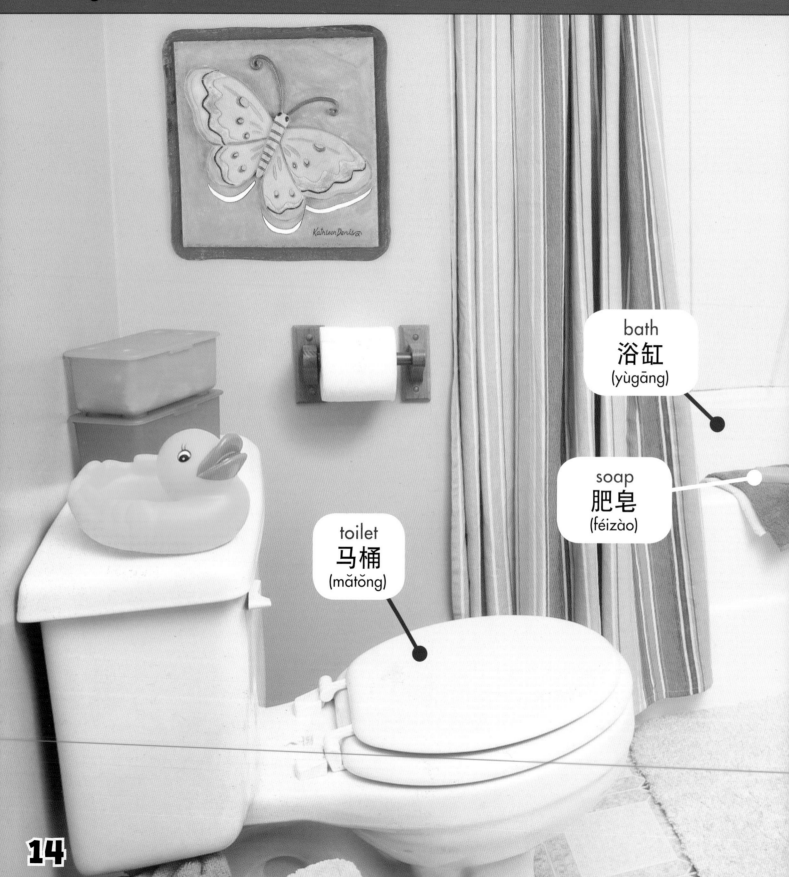

bath
浴缸
(yùgāng)

soap
肥皂
(féizào)

toilet
马桶
(mǎtǒng)

14

mirror
镜子
(jìngzi)

toothbrush
牙刷
(yáshua)

toothpaste
牙膏
(yágāo)

sink
水池
(shuǐchí)

comb
梳子
(shūzi)

towel
毛巾
(máojīn)

brush
刷子
(shuāzi)

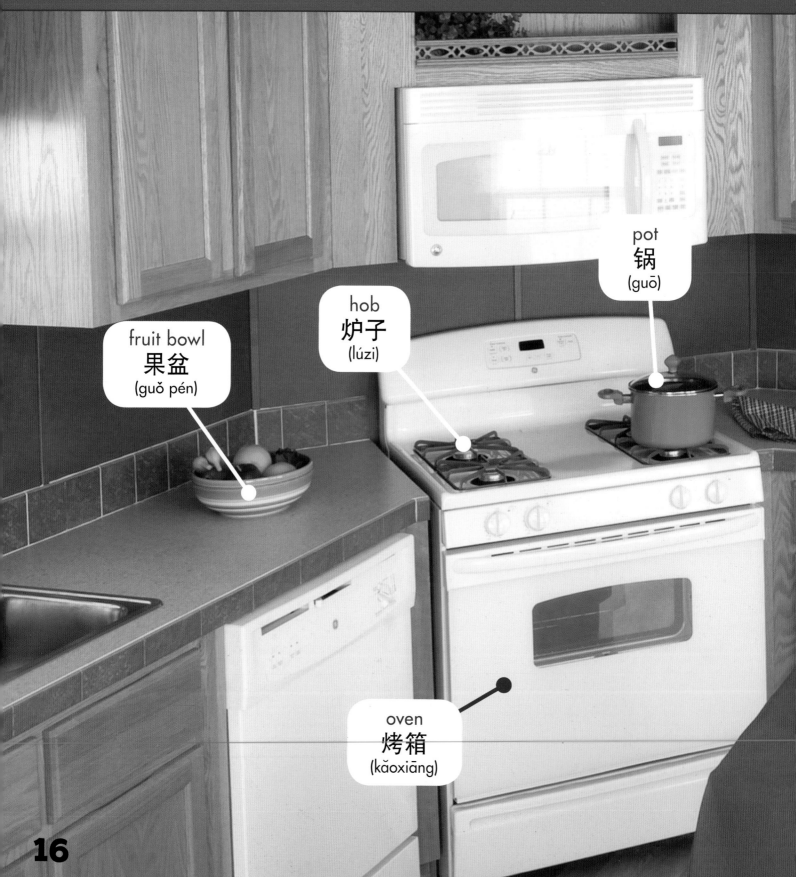

pot
锅
(guō)

hob
炉子
(lúzi)

fruit bowl
果盆
(guǒ pén)

oven
烤箱
(kǎoxiāng)

refrigerator
冰箱
(bīngxiāng)

knife
刀
(dāo)

table
桌子
(zhuōzi)

plate
盘子
(pánzi)

spoon
勺
(sháo)

fork
叉
(chā)

17

milk
牛奶
(niúnǎi)

carrot
胡萝卜
(húluó-bo)

bread
面包
(miànbāo)

apple
苹果
(píngguǒ)

butter
黄油
(huángyóu)

egg
鸡蛋
(jīdàn)

pea
豌豆
(wāndòu)

orange
桔子
(júzi)

sandwich
三明治
(sānmíngzhì)

rice
大米
(dàmǐ)

19

tractor
拖拉机
(tuōlājī)

hay
干草
(gāncǎo)

fence
栅栏
(zhàlán)

farmer
农民
(nóngmín)

sheep
羊
(yáng)

pig
猪
(zhū)

horse
马
(mǎ)

barn
粮仓
(liángcāng)

cow
牛
(niú)

chicken
鸡
(jī)

21

leaf
叶子
(yèzi)

butterfly
蝴蝶
(húdié)

flower
花
(huā)

trowel
铲子
(chǎnzi)

bird
鸟
(niǎo)

worm
虫
(chóng)

plant
植物
(zhíwù)

grass
草
(cǎo)

soil
泥土
(nítǔ)

seed
种子
(zhǒngzi)

23

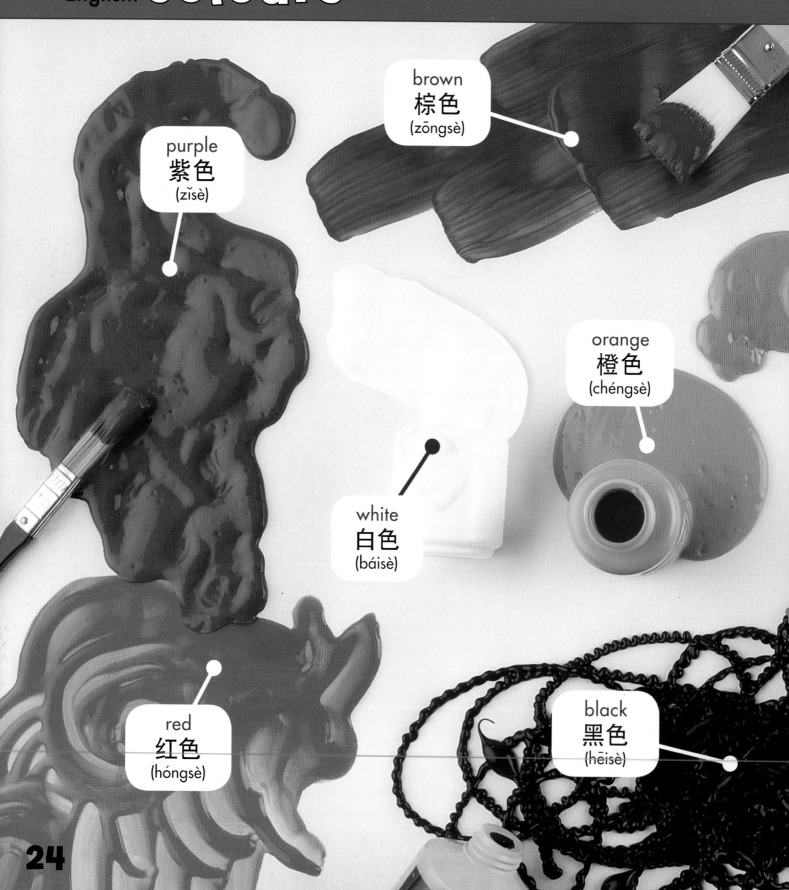

purple
紫色
(zǐsè)

brown
棕色
(zōngsè)

orange
橙色
(chéngsè)

white
白色
(báisè)

red
红色
(hóngsè)

black
黑色
(hēisè)

24

pink
粉色
(fěnsè)

blue
蓝色
(lánsè)

yellow
黄色
(huángsè)

green
绿色
(lǜsè)

25

teacher
老师
(lǎoshī)

book
书
(shū)

crayon
蜡笔
(làbǐ)

pencil
铅笔
(qiānbǐ)

desk
书桌
(shūzhuō)

clock
挂钟
(guàzhōng)

map
地图
(dìtú)

computer
电脑
(diànnǎo)

chair
椅子
(yǐzi)

paper
纸
(zhǐ)

traffic light
红绿灯
(hónglǜdēng)

library
图书馆
(túshūguǎn)

shop
商店
(shāngdiàn)

bicycle
自行车
(zìxíngchē)

car
汽车
(qìchē)

tree
树
(shù)

bus
公共汽车
(gōnggòng qìchē)

park
公园
(gōngyuán)

street
街道
(jiēdào)

sign
标志
(biāozhì)

STOP

29

Numbers • 数字 (shùzì)

1. one • 一 (yī)
2. two • 二 (èr)
3. three • 三 (sān)
4. four • 四 (sì)
5. five • 五 (wǔ)

6. six • 六 (liù)
7. seven • 七 (qī)
8. eight • 八 (bā)
9. nine • 九 (jiǔ)
10. ten • 十 (shí)

Useful phrases • 常用短语 (chángyòng duǎnyǔ)

yes • 是 (shì)

no • 不是 (bù shì)

hello • 你好 (nǐ hǎo)

goodbye • 再见 (zài jiàn)

good morning • 早上好 (zǎoshang hǎo)

goodnight • 晚安 (wǎnān)

please • 请 (qǐng)

thank you • 谢谢 (xièxie)

excuse me • 对不起 (duìbuqǐ)

My name is _____. • 我的名字是 _____. (wǒ de míngzi shì)

Find out more

Look up more Mandarin Chinese words in these books:

Easy Peasy Chinese: Mandarin Chinese for Beginners, Elinor Greenwood (Dorling Kindersley, 2007)

First Thousand Words in Chinese, Heather Amery (Usborne Books, 2014)

Mandarin Chinese Picture Dictionary (Berlitz, 2011)

Websites

Visit these sites to learn more Mandarin Chinese words:

http://www.bbc.co.uk/schools/ primarylanguages/mandarin/

http://www.digitaldialects.com/Chinese.htm

http://fdslive.oup.com/www.oup.com/oxed/children/ firstwords/

Raintree is an imprint of Capstone Global Library Limited, a company incorporated in England and Wales having its registered office at 7 Pilgrim Street, London, EC4V 6LB – Registered company number: 6695582

www.raintree.co.uk
myorders@raintree.co.uk

Designed by Juliette Peters
Picture research by Wanda Winch
Production by Eric Manske
Originated by Capstone Global Library Ltd
Printed and bound in China

ISBN 978 1 474 70688 9 (hardback)
19 18 17 16
10 9 8 7 6 5 4 3 2 1

ISBN 978 1 474 70694 0 (paperback)
20 19 18 17 16
10 9 8 7 6 5 4 3 2 1

British Library Cataloguing in Publication Data
A full catalogue record for this book is available from the British Library.

Acknowledgements
We would like to thank the following for permission to reproduce photographs: Capstone Studio/Gary Sundermeyer, 20 (farmer with tractor, pig); Capstone Studio/Karon Dubke, cover (ball, sock), 1, 3, 4-5, 6-7, 8-9, 10-11, 12-13, 14-15, 16-17, 18-19, 22-23, 24-25, 26-27; Image Farm, back cover, 1, 2, 31, 32 (design elements); iStockphoto/Andrew Gentry, 28 (main street); Photodisc, cover (flower); Shutterstock/Adrian Matthiassen, cover (butterfly); David Hughes, 20 (hay); Eric Isselee, cover (horse), 20-21 (horse); hamurishi, 28 (bike); Ievgeniia Tikhonova, 21 (chickens); Jim Mills, 29 (stop sign); Kelli Westfal, 28 (traffic light); Margo Harrison, 20 (sheep); MaxPhoto, 21 (cow and calf); Melinda Fawver, 29 (bus); Robert Elias, 20-21 (barn, fence); Vladimir Mucibabic, 28-29 (city skyline).

Every effort has been made to contact copyright holders of material reproduced in this book. Any omissions will be rectified in subsequent printings if notice is given to the publisher.

All the internet addresses (URLs) given in this book were valid at the time of going to press. However, due to the dynamic nature of the internet, some addresses may have changed, or sites may have changed or ceased to exist since publication. While the author and publisher regret any inconvenience this may cause readers, no responsibility for any such changes can be accepted by either the author or the publisher.

Note to parents, teachers and librarians

Learning to speak a second language at a young age has been shown to improve overall academic performance, boost problem-solving ability and foster an appreciation for other cultures. Early exposure to language skills provides a strong foundation for other subject areas, including maths and reasoning. Introducing children to a second language can help to lay the groundwork for future academic success and cultural awareness.